What I Like About You

Other  Books

Where's the Cake?:
A Head First Birthday Celebration

What I Like About You

A *Head First* Look at Friendship

Photographs by
JUDY REINEN
with text by
PATRICK REGAN

**Andrews McMeel
Publishing**

Kansas City

ISBN: 0-7407-3633-7

05 06 07 08 09 WKT 10 9 8 7 6 5 4 3 2 1

ATTENTION: SCHOOLS AND BUSINESSES

For: _____

From: _____

Acknowledgments

I want to thank all our magnificent friends from the animal kingdom who allowed me to look into their eyes and preserve their images for generations to enjoy.

I would also like to thank a number of people and organizations that made the Head First portraits possible by their daily work in the preservation of our animal friends.

Alma Park Zoo, Queensland, Australia
Australian Reptile Park, New South Wales, Australia
Currumbin Wildlife Sanctuary, Queensland, Australia
Denver Zoo, Colorado, United States of America
Mogo Zoo, New South Wales, Australia
Stoney Oaks Wildlife Park, New Zealand
Zion Wildlife Gardens, New Zealand
Brenton Bullen, New South Wales, Australia
Karen Hawkyard, New Zealand

Thank you also to the wonderful owners of all the cats, dogs, and domestic animals I photographed. It's great to work with like-minded people who love animals as much as I do!

Furthermore, I feel extremely honored to have been able to photograph each and every animal in the Head First range. I was blown away by the beauty of these animals while viewing them from an extremely close distance—eight inches to be exact! These animals are so important. It makes you realize the extreme value we must place on ensuring their survival.

God bless,

—Judy Reinen, M.Photog NZIPP (2 Gold Bars)

To Anna, Sam, Marco, Kristel, Saskia, Jacob, Sophia, Josiah, and Anysha. Enjoy!

And to my adorable furry animals:
Basil, my faithful dog;
my cats, Oscar, Amigo, Roadie,
Three Spot, and Karl;
and my cute alpacas, Eduardo and Geraldo.

And finally, thanks Mark—
what an awesome journey!

HIYA, buddy!

(Oh, don't act so SURPRISED!)

I've been thinking about what a **LUCKY DOG** I am to have you as a friend.

And—at the risk
of giving you a **BIG HEAD**—

I decided to **TELL YOU**. Ready?

There are so
many things
to like about
a **FRIEND**
like you.

You're **DIGNIFIED** . . .

but **SASSY**.

You have the **WISDOM** of the ages . . .

and the **ENTHUSIASM** of a pup!

You **LAUGH** at my dumb jokes (or at least pretend to),

and when I need to talk, you're **ALL EARS**.

I like you because you stay **CURIOUS**.

Seems like you're always **LOOKING UP** . . . and reaching higher.

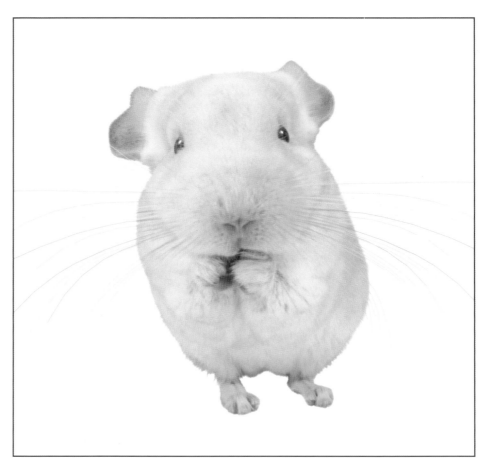

And even though you're **SWEET** as pie,

you have a quiet way of **ASSERTING**
yourself when the need arises.

In times when others **PANIC** . . .

you stay
COOL,
CALM, and
COLLECTED.

When I'm in the **DUMPS** . . .

seeing your **SMILING FACE**
can turn my whole day around.

You make me feel **GOOD** about myself . . .

but **NEVER** let me get *too* uppity.

I like you because you're not a
SLAVE to the latest fashions,

but you *do* have a **STYLE** that's all your own.

And, of course, you have a highly contagious, world-class, 1,000-watt **SMILE**.

I **ADMIRE** you because you meet life head-on,

and you always put your best foot **FORWARD**.

You're **EVERYTHING**
a friend should be: loyal . . .

LAID-BACK . . .

and **LOTS** of laughs.

And even though you're **ALWAYS** ready to offer helpful advice . . .

you don't stick your NOSE in where it doesn't belong.

When I'm feeling **WIPED OUT**,

you help put the **PEP** back in my step.

The simple **TRUTH** is that without you,
I'm not sure if I could face the world.

I know this sounds **CRAZY**, but it's true.

I knew we'd be **FRIENDS** the first time I spotted you.

NO KIDDING!

The **END**.